AND
SHE'S
STILL

Smiling

PUBLISHING

Baton Rouge, LA

Cover Design by: Jade Newell of Jades Graphics

ISBN - 978-0-578-77549-4
EISBN - 978-1-0879-1440-4

Printed and bound in USA

Website: www.pastordomonique.com
Facebook: @domonique.s.washington
Instagram: @pastordomonique

For speaking engagements and booking, email: bookingpastord@gmail.com

AND SHE'S STILL

Smiling

DOMONIQUE S. WASHINGTON

When he
finds me,
I'll be
smiling.

Draw Near

Before our paths cross
See that the light that illuminates
From within
Draws you to me like the star that
Shined above our saviors head
Be lead to me
Like a head to feet
Ordered and aligned

All smiles
I can't wait until he sees that it's a liability to not stick
with me
I'm an asset just by mere existence
The real Him won't be able to lie on my ability to bring
extra to his ordinary view of life and love
I'm the good thing the Bible's been speaking of
When he finds me I'll be smiling because my fairytale
has already started.

Eventually
A word that didn't mean much to me
Until I broke it down completely
Realizing the events that usually
Seemed so far from sight
Now have this progressive view
That leaves them all in view

Tangible in present tense
While I await for them to truly
Exist

Until
The kind of love that surpasses a life time
Forever you're mine
Life with you is time well spent
To have and to hold in hopes of never running out
It's More than having and holding from this day forward
It's that day forward that made this day possible
my new life began when the aisle ended with you
To the end of the row was the end of the road
Boys to men can only understand a decision so priceless all the money couldn't price it
You're my air
No need to acknowledge what I feel
when you are there it's evident
A quivering so deep that only a sigh my mouth does speak

Contents

THE
JOURNEY
Continues

DOMONIQUE S. WASHINGTON

Life Was Not My Fairytale

Growing up, I'd seen countless movies and depictions of love through the lenses of beauty turned ashes turned candlelit celebration. Guy meets Girl. Guy falls in love. Life happens. They forgive each other. Thirty minutes remaining in the film all is well and their ending is blissful. Not until I hit 25, still single, dissatisfied, checking off the stages of grief, and negotiating with God to get back to the "love" part of my story, did I realize the, seemingly unrealistic, expectation I'd placed on myself from those cinematic depictions of love. My life wasn't a movie. I'd gone through the "hard part" of the story, but my 30 minutes turned into several 365 days and my ending wasn't the bliss I anticipated. Because of my obedience to God, my commitment to the process, and my openness to the journey, then my story just had to end "right."

WRONG.

The Story as It Happened

Let me give you somewhat of a brief background to what occurred. Girl and Guy are friends. Guy and Girl heard from God. Girl and Guy enter into a relationship. Guy and Girl decided marriage was the outcome. Guy and Girl stay in a relationship for three years. Guy moves temporarily for work, and Girl has a dream concerning the depths of the separation. Guy stops communicating. Girl seeks God. Girl decides to make clear what's evident. Girl gets answer from God and obeys. Guy moves on, gets engaged, and gets married. Girl? Girl? Girl?

My Truth Got Real

And here we are.

In my mind, I believed my obedience to God would guarantee me an ending to the love part of my story. I would be ready to embrace the life of a woman in ministry with a story to run and tell your girlfriends. But I found myself angry at God. Like, how could He do right by the people who wrong me? Did He not see my heart? Was there no reward for my obedience? Maybe I was being punished. That's it. Because I didn't walk away the first time, maybe I'm single because I'm being punished? Maybe I'm not really healed? Like, I know He worked on me and He healed me, but maybe I just convinced myself of that like all good Christians sometimes do? Maybe my singleness stemmed from the unhealed parts of me that were in in bondage and not ready to be loved?

You name it, I thought it, I asked it, I felt it, and I prayed on it. I just knew that there had to be some reason I was still single! I considered being single like having the plague. I spent so much time trying to fast forward past my singleness that I missed my singleness. I read every book. Watched every sermon. Oh, but I didn't go to the conferences. At a single's meeting I realized my thinking about the nature of singlehood was all wrong. It wasn't the speaker who said it. My wisdom and spirit kicked in, making me realize the purpose attached to this place of singlehood. The more I spoke to singles, the more I realized that my status had become my soapbox. My view of this dreadful place changed. Secretly miserable, I was missing the moment to grow into the woman I thought marriage was going to make me.

My Plan Not His

I am the type of person who plans everything. There were things I wanted to accomplish at certain stages in life. For example, traveling was for the single place, but buying a house was to be with a spouse. No, I didn't intend for that to rhyme; however, it's true. I had envisioned my life through the lenses of my parents, high school sweethearts who married in their late teens. They were *Love and Basketball* and *Brown Sugar*, the best friends who realized they were in love. The church said if I just surrendered, I'd win. I didn't realize I'd added my own idea of winning until later.

But you get the picture.

There was a picture of this love story that I'd played out as a child, teen, and young adult that the woman in me wasn't getting. I didn't have a Plan B, because the plan I had was foolproof. There was no way love and marriage before 30 wasn't my portion. How did I manage to put an age limit as a placeholder for purpose? Since when did I hold the card in my hand to do that? Who was I to think that God had to do it the way I wanted? Who was I to think that God's plan had to function with the terms and conditions of my process?

Thinking about it now I can see the foolishness of my plan.

Growing into Grateful

We all have the idea of our story in mind. The characters, setting, and plot are clear, but very seldom do we plan for what happens beyond the twist. Our timelines bind us in cycles of depression, patterns of frustration, and momentary lapses in judgment trying to create what we saw. That's no way to live.

How can one truly be thankful for life if we are constantly waiting for the day God changes it to something better? What good are we to the process if we are constantly praying for Him to manifest our version of the promise? How ungrateful can we admit we've been by always fasting and seeking more rather than being just grateful for right now? Life in itself is but a vapor and every day we get to live above ground is a blessing.

Where was I really

In this moment of discovery, I decided that single was just another box on my list to check off. It was where I was, in one area, but not who I was. My perspective shifted when I heard God say in a very loud voice, "if I sent him now, you wouldn't even know what to do with him. A "he" will not change the pleasantry of your heart. You need me for that." God shook my entire view with those words. In that moment, I went on a journey to enjoy the life I have the privilege to experience. Singleness may or may not be your choice, but it is an important part of your journey. Through the lenses of this journey, I get the privilege to discover who I am as opposed to what I missed. Getting here did not happen in a day. As penned in previously written books *Lessons from A Good Girl* (2015) and *Ever After Happily* (2018), I've gone through experience after experience to get to this perspective.

You have to pick up the other books to get all the details on the things I learned while walking through this thing called life, but, I tell you, a journey it has been. I have learned things such as the importance of forgiving a friend for unloving and unkind for telling a secret in public—in the middle of a class. A secret between the two of us. Since I could not respond in the way I wanted at the time, I decided to ignore her as if she didn't exist. Only later did I come to understand the pain of being unforgiving to one person brings to other relationships. Learning to forgive, even when someone is wrong, would be important for the later part of my life journey.

At 25, I experienced a heartbreak I would not wish on my enemy. I was left with no understanding of why, how, or what I could have done to go from in love to brokenhearted after what seemed to be three promising years. This began my decision to never be left with the pain of my past and doing whatever it took to have a wholehearted future. I looked at life as this huge open book test for a class I needed to pass to graduate. A conversation with my mentor about enjoying the journey made me realize how much I was trying to create a new path and learn all the lessons at once rather than enjoying the journey. This conversation broadened my view as I understood life is not only about learning those valuable lessons that shape us into who we are but enjoying the process along the way.

My Heart's Desire

During the first Woman Evolve Conference, Sarah Jakes Roberts, moderating a panel on being and becoming a woman of God, asked each panelist, "What did you lose in order to become?" Me, being the creative that I am, always watch these type of interviews as if I'm sitting on the stage and I decided to answer the question for myself. "Domonique, what did you lose in order to become?"

It hit me.

I had to rid myself of my fairytale. The young girl in me desired to become a married woman, with kids and a beautiful home, all before 30. She had passion and platforms, traveling the world and effected a change through God that only she could. Her family and friends love and respected her.

She was It.

Everyone wanted to be her, and her daughter couldn't wait to become her. I dreamed of this woman. I envisioned her on stages and filling rooms with her class and wit. I desired more than anything to embrace her. So, I fought to obey God and seek Him to manifest her. She was the woman I was after. She was the woman I just had to meet.

Then, the big breakup happened when I was 25. This was not just any breakup. This was the breakup of all breakups. I thought this was the relationship that would put an end to looking for any other relationships. Having been together for three long years and having this "perfect" love story only to realize we were at a point of no return. The flags I saw were real, and the guy I loved had slipped away. I could do nothing else to regain our footing because I had to accept that I may have been the only one making an attempt toward the end goal I thought we were both seeking. So, after several months, I decided to accept the inevitable truth of letting go and moving on. This pain left me not only wearing black all of the time, and going from a size 8 to a size 2, but it also broke down the blissful hopeless romantic into a woman that, probably for the first time, saw the world in a way she never imagined she would. People could hurt you after having made a commitment to love you. They can search for rings and later search for excuses to not honor what their mouth and former actions said they would. In this heartache, I had lost her, the "her" in me, my passion, my perspective. Not that I wanted to lose her, but pain had ripped a whole in my story and now my fight was different. My fight was to hold on tight to her and find a partner to recreate the vision I saw in my head. I was single, hurting, and holding on to the fairytale heartbreak was trying to rip from me. I was a new me, and I didn't like it. The me I had become seemed to contradict the fairytale in my head, and I was angry. How could I get to this place? The me that obeys has to embrace this woman that seemed so intolerant.

Pain birthed this newness of purpose that wasn't a part of my original story. I became the advocate for singles and the voice of women in ministry. I surpassed just being the kind-hearted lady who was great with kids and able to reach young adults. A teacher by profession and a youth pastor in ministry. But my pain seemed to give me a twist in the tale.

So, I fought her.

I hated her boldness and rejected her newfound zeal to be open and transparent about things the pre-pain me wouldn't have dared utter, and then, it dawned on me. What will happen if I stop being miserable about who I'd become and get to know the me God was trying to manifest. I looked in the mirror and said goodbye the fairytale I once knew and said, "God grow me into the woman you can use."

When I stopped being miserable, I realized all the pieces I needed to become the fairytale still existed. I learned to love the path purpose produced even if it looked nothing like the path I expected. I would never get a chance to know the woman I had become if I continued to live my life in regret. There was beauty beyond my relationship status, and I was determined to see it everywhere I could.

So, I coined the hashtag/phrase "And when he finds me, I'll be smiling."

I'd done some research on the powerful effects of smiling. There are several studies proving that smiles are powerful enough to change your weight and clothing size. No, seriously. You can google it and find its truth. Behavioral psychologist Sarah Stevenson writes in her blog, "Magic in Your Smile," that each time you smile, you throw a little feel-good party in your brain." The endorphins come together and actual create a sense of well-being in your mood. I figured I could do better for myself, with my smile, both literally and figuratively. I just needed to make the conscious effort to find the God in this life even if, some days, I had trouble seeing the good. Because, in reality, being single and waiting isn't all girls' trips and free money no more than it is a lifetime of doom and gloom.

But yes, sometimes, single sucks. I recall this time of making light of being single after trying to take up the groceries after leg day at the gym. At the time, I lived in a one-bedroom apartment on the second floor. I was so annoyed that not only did I have to walk up those stairs by myself, but I also had to figure out how I could bring up several bags of groceries in one trip. Following this moment. I went to Facebook and penned, what became "Don't complain about being single when you have to get up in the middle of the night to turn off the light. Complain about being single when you have to bring several bags of groceries upstairs after leg day." I try to make light of the moments, but in real life, on lonely days and cold nights, single will suck. Other times single is a relief. Getting up and going out of town without having to clear it with anyone else, or making a big purchase because it's your money and you worked hard for the random bag you saved for. The view of single is all in the day and mind. But what I desire for us singles is that we find more reasons to smile regardless of what isn't happening for us on the relationship front.

One day, I was sitting with my best friend and talking about our singlehood. Earlier, someone asked me how I handle being single and being in ministry. For whatever reason, people seem to think that my life in the fishbowl as giving me the DM's of gold, and I just hit the jackpot in the male category. In that moment of enlightenment, I thought it was about time for someone to shed a little reality on the blissfulness of being single, satisfied, and waiting to be sought out.

With this book I decided to take you through the beautiful twists and turns of being single and collecting data. Through my journey of learning how to operate in singleness from the lessons learned while on my way and encounters of others seeking guidance and encouragement while on theirs. It is my hope to both enlighten and encourage you to enjoy them all. You are not wrong for desiring a spouse. But we are wrong if we consider traveling the same route and expecting to get to a new destination. This time we want to explore every phase in life from the eyes of love, enlightenment, and lessons. We are not just seeking out our perfect mate but learning to be the perfect mate that we hope they are seeking while just learning to enjoy the journey even if there are a few bumps along the way. Dating, collecting data as I will refer to it throughout the book, can be an exciting and teaching experience if done from a place of an open mind to the process and a heart connected to God.

I just want you to realize you can smile and be sought after at the same time. Some conversations concerning enjoying singlehood and collecting data will have you recreating the life of bliss view in a new way.

DON'T LET THE WAIT FOOL

—You

DOMONIQUE S. WASHINGTON

Before we get into the heart of the matter, I want to state the obvious. Let's just be real. Time after time, we hear how we should be happy about being single. This idea can cause us to become super critical of ourselves. Well, let me be saved, single and honest. Waiting for "your turn" can feel like an eternity. Especially if you've had to be single and supportive. You know, be the sister planning the wedding, or the friend hosting the shower. Oh, and don't let me forget, the babysitter for Valentine's Day. I remember feeling like I was the prayer warrior that could get to the ears of God for everyone else— except myself. It seemed that the only relationship I was going to get to have is the one I lived vicariously through with those around me. I've drawn the conclusion that I only found myself at that frame of thinking because when someone told me I had "next," I translated it to mean "soon." The joke, then, seemed to be on me because there I was still single and still waiting while still supporting everyone else. That was, until this random day for a scheduled oil changed everything.

Oil Changed My Ways

One of those single things I hate to do is taking care of my car. It's a time commitment, to say the least, so I plan and prepare for getting my car service. Well, the day had finally come where I'd set out to take care of my car. I'm up, showered, and out of the house with time to spare. I stop for a cup of coffee (who does life without coffee?), and I'm in line and ready to be checked in by the mechanic. The line is oddly long, but I'm patiently waiting my turn. It's finally my turn, and I let the attendant know that I fulfilled the option of making an appointment online. You see, the online appointments were said to be more promising than just driving up. So, this was my way of letting him know to be sure I'm awarded some type of special treatment for planning ahead. I walk in only to find several people awaiting their vehicles' return. I'm subconsciously believing God that they hadn't followed the rules. Hey, think what you must, but sitting in a dealership on a Saturday morning isn't high on the list of exciting things to do. Well, just as I was believing God, I looked around and realized I'd be in for a wait. Hopefully, not a long wait, but a wait indeed.

A Wait Indeed

I sat there watching the little boy next to me play with his toys. I smile, and his mom lets me know how proud she is because they'd been waiting for some time for their repair to be done and he was being good. As I watched this kid patiently wait for his mom's car to arrive, I realized three very simple, yet important things.

1. Your wait isn't **average**. Your wait is by God's design.

2. You're not **alone**. Your wait will make you feel like you're the only one in your situation, but honestly, you're not the only one in the world! It's your journey, but someone shares your path. Meet the others in the room and connect with a tribe of like-minded others.

3. You have **assignments** to complete while you're waiting.

While I'm Waiting

While waiting I decided to distract myself with some music, reading, social media surfing, and then it happened. That moment you look around and realize the line isn't moving, and it's already been over an hour. Trying to assure God that I've learned my lesson on patience, I redo the things I've already done and adjust my posture. I figure I needed to look "happy" about waiting and maybe GOD WOULD BELIEVE I was being a good student. Don't judge me. I look at my watch, and though it is approaching the two-hour mark, I decide to just stop it.

Just Stop It

Watching the clock wasn't helping at all. In fact, watching the clock caused my anxiety. Paying attention to how long it had been was making me feel as if the waiting was more dreadful than it was. I then asked myself these three questions:

1.   What am I missing?
2.   What am I losing?
3.   What am I doing?

Questions That Need Answers

The first question, "What am I missing?" felt loaded and twofold. The first thing I asked was, "Was my waiting really causing me to miss out on anything? Listen, it was a Saturday morning, but I had no other plans that couldn't wait. Everything I had planned to do can still be done after everything was completed. There wasn't a dire need to rush. But is there ever? Is this wait really causing some clock to dictate your fate? I've read countless stories about women who beat the odds of that ticking clock. So, is that really a reason to rush? Is it really? I started to really answer this question from different views. Maybe God was saving me from something I couldn't see. Could this time be used for something life hadn't given me a chance to do because I'd been too busy or too distracted by something I couldn't control?

The second part of this question was, "What am I missing out on because I'm focused on what's missing in my life?" Being so focused on the time passing as a loss, I didn't see it as a win for finally bringing this book to a close. I was finally able to sit down and catch up on reading. Finally, I could hear my own thoughts. This led me to also question, "What am I losing? What am I losing out on seeing, doing, or becoming because I'm worried about the clock?" Wouldn't it be a shame to be upset about time passing only to realize all you allowed yourself to do was watch time pass?

There is a life that can be lived while the clock ticks. Experiences that can be embraced by the seconds, minutes, and even hours while the clock ticks. I asked myself, what are you going to do? What in the heck am I doing now? Do I continue to complain about the time, or do I live and cover so much ground with the time given that when my clock runs out, I'll hear, "You done good!" And I finally realized I was being fooled by the wait.

Don't Miss the Time

The wait will have you thinking you're missing out on so much that you actually do end up missing out. You will miss life and just miss the chance to be open enough for life to teach, grow, and produce something in you that without the time allotted you wouldn't have otherwise done. Just a few seconds after this big "wow" moment, I heard, "Miss Washington, your car is ready." I was so engulfed with using my time wisely that I hadn't focused on the fact that during the wait my name was called. That's right, it was my turn to step to the desk and pay my tab. He handed me my keys, and I was headed up and out.

That's a word right there.

While I was working my wait and not concerned with the time, my turn showed up! Darling, don't let the allotted time make you miss out on living because it took longer than expected. You will get your turn in your appointed time.

Single isn't all bad no more than it is all good. Sometimes single sucks. I know I've said that before, but I just want you to know that it's ok to literally want out some days. Then there are other times that single is the best company to ever have stock in. You don't have to answer to anyone. You can eat your last crumb without sharing, reluctantly or not.. Oh, but on the first of the month that two income household sounds like a win. The way I see it, the GENERAL idea of single shouldn't be terrible or dreadful and yet the DAILY idea of single must come from some self-awareness.

I Know Me Well Enough

Getting to a place where I became aware of my triggers while losing my timeline took effort. I prayed to God to forget old calendar dates such as, the day he broke my heart, the last date we went on, or something as simple as birthdays and makeshift anniversaries etc. became prayer requests It may seem a bit drastic, but the calendar dates we remember can easily become the days we prepare to get hit by. Let's be honest, when the relationship is over, it's the dates we won't allow ourselves to forget that keep us connected to the place we are no longer in relation with.

How Soon Do We Forget?

In college, I didn't hide my light. There were times when others would connect me to people in a dark place that needed my light. One of those people was a girl who experienced tragedy and heartache most of her life. When she learned I was a minister, she opened her heart to me. The more she talked, the more I realized she was the source of her own pain. She had depressed dates down to a science. She would text me on Monday letting me know she would be depressed on Thursday. No, I'm serious. Every calendar date of every high and low of her life was etched in her brain.

Even days that should be considered celebratory moments had negative connotations. For instance, her mother's birthday was a depressed date because of her mother's death. She rehearsed these calendar dates so much that her subconscious even knew how to respond with little to no effort. You see, that's the way the brain works. Your brain literally tells your body, "Hey guys, this is how we respond when she's in this situation, so prepare for breakdown." So, in the same way, year after year, her body, mind and heart went into autopilot, and those dates controlled her life.

During my time of connection with her, my goal was to help her break the pattern of negative anticipation and disconnect from the negativity so she could better enjoy and appreciate the present and celebrate the past. As I became mindful of my own triggers, God reminded me of my time with her. God showed me how I had already gone through my training station on how to think about what I am thinking about. So, I asked God to show me myself, to open my eyes to how I handled the pain and trials I experienced in love and relationships. To help me get to a place of not lugging the stint of what didn't or hasn't happened yet with me in a negative and overbearing way. I even asked for him to show me the areas of my emotional and mental state and where I am my own hazard. Listen, this prayer request and thought process is not for the faint of heart. I needed to be courageous enough to see me as I really am. It's not always easy looking at yourself in the mirror. Not the filter image, but the true visual of who you are and what you've gotten yourself into.

Accepting My Truth

Man, I just couldn't believe how much of the pain I experienced was my own fault. I mean, of course I wasn't self-loathing and solely blaming myself. I did, however, admit that I wasn't independently innocent. There were some obvious insecurities I picked up on this journey through life. Those things that once brought me joy and excitement had somehow become dreadful and mentally exhausting. I was no longer excited about being the bridge. The bridge had become a barrier. Realizing this truth was tough for me. I knew I loved who God had created me to be as a conduit for enlightenment, but there had to be a reason, something, or someone that brought about this change in me.

At this point, I had to have some harsh conversations with myself and admit some things about me that many probably never will. You see, it was always my goal, when I approached this healing process following heartache, to not just cope, but to become whole. I made a vow to be willing to face, accept, and do whatever God and a therapist said was necessary for me to COMPLETLEY whole. I saw what coping looked like. I encountered and counseled those who looked healed but struggled behind closed doors. I didn't want that. I didn't want to preach healing but live broken. For me, that meant facing the hard truths and doing the real work. This was one of those moments. Looking at myself and asking: Hey why are you recalling calendar dates? Why are you still connected socially with people who update you to his whereabouts and those details that are no longer necessary for your personal life? Why are you still holding on to a place you say you want to break free from? Of course, I had justifiable excuses. Things like, I spent a lot of time there. I had invested and I deserved this and that or, my all-time favorite, how can I forget things that had, at one point, meant so much to me? After I finished my rant, God asked a simple yet powerful question, "Do you want to be made whole?" This one took me by surprise, not because it was a hard question to answer, but because I remembered making a vow to do whatever it would take to be whole. So, I decided to get past all the reasons holding me back and make the conscious effort to be intentional about moving forward.

I searched in scripture asking God to create in me a clean heart, and if that meant removing dates, such as the dates we once celebrated, first date, the day he asked me to be his girl, etc., then so be it. I no longer needed or wanted to be attached to things from my past that harmed my present. I didn't want calculated dates and planned depression. Dates that were once celebrated can be the ones that you mourn. I wanted to be free and made new. During this process, I realized the harshness of my present state was tied to my mental place. I had to get intentional about my thoughts, actions, and emotions.

Now, I'm sure you are thinking that emotions aren't yours for the choosing, but they are. We can control our emotions. We can determine how long we allow something to stay with us. We can determine how long we focus on a day and time. You may not be like me and legitimately forget certain things until asked, but you can determine how long you will stay in that memory. Harsh or light can be determined by you. In the words of my great God, "Choose ye this day."

DOMONIQUE S. WASHINGTON

NO RULES
JUST
Engagement

DOMONIQUE S. WASHINGTON

Growing up, I watched a lot of the good television shows. Representation wasn't plentiful, but it was purposeful. Shows like *The Cosby Show*, *The Fresh Prince*, *Family Matters*, and *A Different World* were powerful references of what it looked like to be successful, family-oriented, and cool in a black family. You could literally turn on the television on Friday night and see yourself moving and flowing in America whatever your situation was. I don't know about you, but it wasn't until *A Different World* that I envisioned College Life and graduation. Those were just a few of the shows to smile back and YouTube to get a break from the Reality TV era. Yes, we do need a break from scripted "real" tv, but I digress. While writing this book, I started to think about what representation I saw of being black, successful, dating, yet single in America then it hit me, *Living Single*. (Please tell me you're old enough to smile thinking of the cast and if you're not, Hulu it and thank me later.) *Living Single*, embodied trying to navigate life and love while giving you the reality of what single and successful could look like. I miss having television shows that gave a more well-rounded view of this process. You didn't just see an instant fairytale wedding or toxic marriage. You saw the ins and outs of collecting data and trying to make this dating thing work for you, of how to make life work for you. There were lessons displayed by viewing the possibility of reality not being pleasurable. You learned amid being entertained. You grew in perspective by viewing a script that portrayed more than a glamourous side of life; that is, if you choose to be open to take the scripted television and place it against the reality we are now presented with. There seem to be more principles being plugged in on "how to get through" than a simple formula of how to "make just like," as folks say.

What Formula?

The issue I've found with today's dating world is that many like to pass off this "formula" for success then we find ourselves buying into believing that if I just pray the same prayer Ciara prayed, then a Russell will fall into my lap. Jada Pinkett Smith's *Red Table Talk* gave a glimpse into the truth behind her "real" journey. Social media gives us this buy in to our "best" picture that I think many of us forget. There's a process to everything. There are a few who seemed to just land a prince, but in true fairytale fashion, a few things happened along the way to be in the right position to reach the happy ending. In the words of Bishop T.D. Jakes, "Nothing Just happens." Everything worth having takes some time to get to. Yes, we have easier ways to prepare meals, but only because someone else went before us and did the heavy work. You have to be willing to set a firm foundation and then build to have a house, or should I say relationship, worth living in for years to come. Love and relationships are not a ready-made dish. Can you just consider that even with the formula of another your situation may require something different?

Foundation Set

I don't want you to feel bad if you've ever secretly or openly desired to get your hands on the Ciara prayer. Let's just be honest here. At some point in life we have scrutinized the successes of others and wondered if they would share the ingredients to the secret sauce. I've told you how I went on a quest to figure out how I can be more relationship ready. I'd seen relationships flourish from my advice and then it not work for me. Just as I've witnessed a former coworker marry and remarry three times as I remained single the entire time. I'm not talking the new age, "I got a boo without a title" single. I've been the no date, no convo, dry DM single. Yes, you can laugh. Even I chuckled. What's my point? My point is that we have all been in a season, phase, time of wanting to figure out where we were going wrong and what we can get right.

Soul searching is important. It is vital to know yourself well enough to know where you need to grow, heal and let go. I am a firm believer and in full agreeance of Dr. Myles Munroe statement that, "your marriage is only as good as your individual." Your relationship will require a healed, whole and solid version of yourself in order to sustain those qualities in your relationship. So, yes, seek out your flaws and know them well. Find your faults and get them fixed. Come to grips with the things about you that ruined your failed relationship and grow as much as you can. We all fall short in one way or another. Even I, as I write this book, can recall a time when I realized one of my flaws was learning to express how I felt and not assume that people should automatically know when I was hurt or offended. I had to adjust my view of confrontation. I was so afraid to openly confront others that I was creating self-afflicting wounds by not voicing my feelings or my hurts. This created unnecessary friction and tension in past relationships People can only adjust in places that they know need to be adjusted. You can't hold something against another that they had no clue was even an issue. I, too, had to make the necessary effort to grow as a person in order to experience growth in my relationships. So, there was no way that I could truly accept the hype that singleness was caused by some lack of effort on my part. I was doing the work. I was making the changes. I was growing and open to change. And like me, if you have done the necessary efforts to correct and consider don't accept that you're single because you didn't do something someone else did. Your story isn't theirs. The basis by which a story is written will be the same. There are titles, character and settings that will all be needed to build a great foundation, but the names, genres, climax and plot twist won't be. Compatibility, chemistry, like mindedness, similarity is intent, desire future endeavors and purpose are vital to your foundation for a strong relationship. But you won't have Boaz, Russel, or Joseph. Those men are married. No, real talk. We look at them and want one just like it, but in reality, what God has for you probably won't look like the one he has for her. We live in a time where we want a Russell, not a Scooter. Ok. Follow me. I'm taking you back to *Living Single.* Scooter was Khadijah's best friend, turned boyfriend, turned ex, turned long distance lover, turned fiancé, and back to friend again. Russell, "appeared to be" this knight in shining armor sent to rescue the broken damsel in limelight and love her back to life, both relationships took obvious work. Only one of them demonstrated the effort we were able to fully see through. Whether it's the highlight reel of present or the sitcom reel of old, all relationships have a foundation. It's up to you to be willing to do the work to determine if that foundation will be solid or shaky. I don't know about you, but I'll take solid over shaky any day.

Let's just be honest. There are many of us who know or have experienced a shaky foundation. It appeared to be solid. It appealed to the eye. Other people would see it and marvel at it's beautiful hashtags and like the pictures. There is patchwork being done behind the screen of social media to fix the issues present. Patchwork only last for so long. At some point, we must come to grips with the reality of our start up and realize until the foundation is fixed the patch work will always be needed. Let's work to build relationships that not only look strong but are strong. When I think of a strong relationship I think from the following acronym: S.T.R.O.N.G.

Stepping toward the desired end
Taking the necessary pauses to explore concerns
Remembering to strengthen the individual
Observing the joys of the journey
Navigating with God and wise others
Going in the flow of a healthy together

Your ability to see beyond the tags and pictures allows you the chance to not be taken aback by the work that you will encounter to maintain the strength of your story. All is well that does the work to maintain sickness and health. Ask yourself this question, *"Do I know how I want my ship to be designed before I board?"*

What Does Success Look Like?

As a single, it is important for you to know what you consider a successful relationship. What does it need for you to sustain, maintain, and enjoy it? Where did you gain this idea? Have you seen what you are looking for play out in real life? Do you have access to anyone who will help you achieve this image? I know I have asked a plethora of questions but intentionally so.

When we can answer the where, why, and how we plan to get to our view of success, then we can maintain the work that it will take to get there as well as give insight to why we even desire it in the first place. It will, in fact, help us to see if there is even healthiness in the foundation by which we are even building the idea. For example, if you say, "I want to be married because no one else in my family is married," you run the risk of staying in an unhealthy relationship because your why is for status, not sustainability. Now, I'm not saying that this is a matter of fact consequence to that reasoning; however, I am saying that in knowing that to be your why and realizing that as your truth than you can look back and see where you may need to add to your purpose in an effort to ensure there is growth and healthiness being built. Without a clear "why," you run the risk of entering patterns and behaviors that will have you surviving in pain instead of living in purpose. For everything, there is a reason by which it exists, and your relationships are not exempt.

When I say relationships, I don't just mean romantically. I think that's where some of us miss it. We think that success in our romantic relationships isn't reflected in our other "ships." How we choose to handle our other 'ships, i.e. friendships, partnerships, etc., play a big part in how we will handle the different phases of our romantic relationships. You see, true love grows beyond feelings. It is, in essence, something that the entirety of your being is supposed to experience.

Biblically speaking, we not only see love as passion through Solomon, but we see love as pain and sacrifice through Christ. We marvel at John Legend saying that "all of me loves all of you," but have you really considered that "ALL" of you has to be present when true love shows up? This means that the "who" you are in the compartments shows up in the face of the one with whom you make a covenant. When you move beyond the fairytale, the reality of who you are is at the core of your being that will begin to shape your story. Yes, the hidden expectations you have for a spouse, your career, family, and even finances are all present when you relate one to another in covenant. I always advise that we use the single years as the growing and training station. In my single days, with my closest friends, is where I can work through my self- centeredness and even an inability to consistently communicate. My procrastination on the job is where I can learn to prioritize for a future life of a professional and married woman. It's in the current space that we are in that prepares us for the space we are traveling toward.

The misconception that nouns, (person, place things and ideas) will automatically fall into place without consideration of how one functions with self and with others etc. leaves many unprepared. There's a level of vulnerability and truth of who are and who you have always been that shows up at the moment of wanting to truly connect and build a life with another. It's in the closeness of that level of relating that allows a person to SEE all of who you are. Think about how rare that is for many of us. On Sunday, your church friends see your "church" you. Monday through Friday your work friends see your "work" you. On Saturday your close friends see the "chill" you. You encounter a partner that will not get to see you in compartments and momentary spaces, but in fullness. WOW! That is major right?

Ok, now, consider the depth of that and then think of how you face it without having an idea of what you want, who you want it with and what it will take to get there. Yes, it's that serious. I am not trying to minimize the fun of love, but I do want you to have an open mind to see that beauty is not shallow and surface. There will be beauty in the deep end too because you had just a glimpse of knowing it was just beyond where the sand no longer touched your toes.

Strategy to Successful Engagement

You may be feeling like I just threw you in the ocean from a plane like a navy seal, considering all the things I have asked you to open your mind to. The idea of relating to another on that level can seem massive and intimidating. Listen, while all the above are true for relationship building, do not allow it to discourage you from a relationship budding.

You have, or can have, what it takes to sustain the relationship you are seeking, but you must be willing to remain active in growing, evolving, and changing and being sure to connect with someone that is willing to go through the evolution and revolution with you. Success is not solely on what is happening in the now but must consider and be open to what is yet to come. When we connect with another, it is not just for where we are, but also for where we are going. Engaging with another is the only way to set a ship in motion. A ship is just a display without its ability to float in the water. Just as every ocean will have a different set of waves at different times, days, and seasons, a ship still requires the same basic set of engagement to set sail. You may board different ships, but ultimately the objective of interacting from a healthy space via communication, consistency, closeness, and even conflict, is possible. Foundationally, your eye is on the why, structurally your interactions are on the now, and later all the while spiritually, emotionally, and mentally you are striving to weed through the things that are unhealthy, grow toward the things that are healthy, and build as often as possible to maintain and sustain a successful you for a powerful "we". Don't just set out on a whim to enjoy the ride. Strategize and seek out an arrangement that will ensure transformative lessons and abundantly living while interacting in life with like-minded others.

When I think of strategy in this regard, I am not talking sitting and complying an InstaPot recipe of things you can place in a pot, leave on the stove for thirty minutes, and viola your perfect relationship is done. No, this time I am asking you to explore your inner self and know how you are in every area of interaction and being influenced by others and determine to find areas of satisfaction, highs, lows and growth spots to encounter solely before and while budding a relational encounter with others. You aren't just what you eat. You become where you engage with great effort. Just as there are two sides to every story there are several encounters by two individuals when attempting to take a solo act and make it a duo. The cohesion of the duo is determined by the compliments of the one. The better you can move in your compartments the more room and steps you must add to your covenant. So, take a deep breath, open your eyes, get rid of the rules while being sure of your needs and simply engage. Occupy, attract, and involve someone's interest and attention by knowing YOU.

DOMONIQUE S. WASHINGTON

TERMS
AND
Conditions

DOMONIQUE S. WASHINGTON

Oftentimes, what I do for God allows me an opportunity to encounter souls in search of a heart of compassion. This places me in situations to be a good listener in hopes of offering some form of comfort and counsel to those lost and in search of redemption. I recall a conversation that I had with a young woman fighting depression. This wasn't an ordinary depression, if that is even a thing. This depression came from matters of the heart. It resonated with me because I knew what it was like to be her. To be in search of any answers that can bring a sense of peace to a giant hole in the heart that seemed would never close. Someone or something that can look at all of the questions you bring to the table and solve the jigsaw puzzle of confusion and bring sense to it. When I heard her story, so many common truths unfolded. I quickly informed her she wasn't the only person to have become privy to these truths. The first thing I decided to do was let her know that she wasn't alone. As human beings we can find ourselves in situations that will seem like an isolated incident to us. Because things happen to us it can seem that it is only us. The world is so big, but it isn't that big. Ecclesiastes 1:9 says, "What has been is what will be, and what has been done is what will be done, and there is nothing new under the sun." When I grew older, the phrase made more sense than a little bit. The day, time, and person may be different, but, oftentimes, the basics of the incidents are the same. As I continued to listen to her story, I was able to pull out data that seem too common, too often. I listened as she revealed a truth that I knew I needed to address with the hearts I have yet to encounter soon enough. I was determined to store this data, knowing it would come in handy one day soon in hopes to broaden the perspective and prepare the eyes of others to beware of this truth.

You see, the young woman did something that if you haven't done it, you can name at least two people who have. She heard a man say that he wasn't ready for anything serious, and yet, because of his willingness to continue to engage and connect with her somewhere along their journey, she determined in her mind that maybe she can continue to be the "difference." She would be the one to change his mind. This was her metamorphosis into BECOMING, and she had no clue that it was taking place before she was head over hills entangled with the idea of forever and longer than a moment with him.

Who Did You Bring to the Table?

Without awareness or even a need to see an issue with her stance, she BECAME everything he said he wanted. She didn't present him with anything that was "her" that would interrupt her chances of being the difference he seemed to enjoy. She was hoping to get him by being the "her" he would mention in the vulnerability conversation. This can often happen unbeknownst to the heart in longing. It is so easy to only present the pleasurable things when trying to connect passionately and permanently with another. Look at it like taking twenty selfies only to decide to post the ONE that you think will rank in the likes. It is the highlight reel presentation that we are subconsciously drawn to. Do not beat yourself up, but please consider this to be a truth to notice. During the phase of identifying that you are indeed interested in collecting data from another, you must be sure to create pause moments to be sure that the real you is at the table of deliberation. Not the you that will continue to be enticing and appealing, but the you that will be left in this connection for the long haul.

Sincerely ask yourself, "AM I HERE?" Not in the literal sense of enjoying the moment or being self-aware, but in the literal sense of being unashamed in who you are, what you carry, what you desire and the things by which you are just NOT ok with or without. This is an important practice to have in place during the dating process. Important because you don't want to look up and find yourself unhappy and wrapped up in a relationship that, if not being led by desire, you probably wouldn't be in it.

Been There. Done That

I was conversing with this guy, for the second time around. Doing my due diligence to give him another chance to be ready and available, as years had passed, and we had both grown and matured. I was not the woman he interacted with years ago. The sassy and bold Domonique he met this time differed greatly from the Domonique he knew. He found the woman I had matured into more vocal and less passive on non-negotiables and future plans.

Knowing these truths and continuing the path of collecting data, we proceeded to converse. As time went on, I began to see things I knew I was not okay with, and I voiced it immediately. Nothing major, but the passive me did not exist anymore, so the old school idea of a "kept woman" just was not it. He called it having a "mouth" while I called it using my voice. Mouthy to him was simply me having my own opinion about things that concerned me and not just doing or saying something because he said I shouldn't. For instances, I already had a job, so him telling me that if we remained together, I had to quit my job needed to be more of a discussion than a demand. Communication is a nonnegotiable for me. Not just that he had to call and talk to me, but that we needed to communicate, to discuss issues and not just assume or make demands. Never disrespectful on either part but clashing more than before because the matured Domonique was at this table. We hit a few snags and had a few high's, but I later vocalized that the woman he wanted and the man I needed was not going to be found in our union. There were just some things I determined that did not line up with who I now was emotionally, psychologically, and spiritually and where I was going in those same areas.

At first, it was the idea of him having a timeline of getting down the aisle because he was "ready" that almost made me waver in bringing ME to the table. I quickly realized I had already been there and done that. Initially timid about speaking my truth out of the fear that this would be my last chance down the aisle, I was quickly reminded that I had made a vow to never go back to that place, and/or, be that woman. Yes, I needed to be honest, and truth be told, so did he.

Make Yourself Known

Truth be told, I had forgotten about this encounter, to this extent, until I saw tears stream down the young woman's face. You see, she revealed to me that after bringing in the data of sexual activity to their union, things changed.

The more we talked, the more I realized that it was not things that changed, but the She that showed up. The intimacy of sex made her relaxed. So relaxed that she stopped becoming what he wanted and began to be who she was. She was being herself because she felt safe enough to do so. Oh, but therein lies the problem. The woman at the table confused him. To him, she had changed. She was not the woman he described as wanting. No, she was altogether something different. Her voice was different. How she responded to his quirks was no longer pleasurable. He began to look at her like "who is this woman" all the while she was screaming "I'm me."

The Space You Want

Her need for a seat at "a" table allowed her to make space at the available table before checking the menu or determining if this was even a table she wanted to sit at. There was a time when you actually learned what was on the menu when you were at the restaurant. Nowadays, you can read reviews on Google, Instagram, Yelp.

Everything is, literally, at your fingertips. What are you saying? Use your access to data before you decide that you "HAVE TO" take a seat at a table simply because there is an availability to do so.

She was so desperate, without fault, to have a chair pulled out and offered a seat that she was too afraid to say what she wanted out of fear that she would not be the "she" he needed. She failed to look at the very fact that who you are goes with you into a relationship well before you ever enter it. My take is, you may as well put it ALL on the table, especially if it is the table by which you plan on building your life around. The fear factor is a dangerous condition to bring into your dating scene, especially if that fear is not a reverence or respect for God, yourself, or your values. If you bring fear to the data point (the idea of alone, lonely, age, biological clocks, etc.), then it will cause more harm than good.

As I said in my book, *Ever After Happily*, do not let lack lead you. If you lead with the idea of this data agent being your only hope, then you will, in fact, find yourself functioning from a compromising position. I kid you not. Compromise shows up at the place of fear of "never again." It's reality functioning from that place simply means that you lack faith and have lost hope. It is that form of desperation that leaves you with the idea that "I have to date him" because there may never be another. You do not have to accept **EVERYTHING** just because you don't have **ANYTHING**.

Hold Your Values

I titled this chapter "Terms and Conditions" to address, the frequent elephant in the room--your values. "Terms and Conditions" is defined as an agreement between a service provider and person who wants to use that service. In the case of this book, the Terms and Conditions are the set of beliefs, values, ideas, and functions by which one can live by when deciding to come into a relational agreement between another. This seems to be the place by which people waver and, in my opinion, is the place that wavering should least likely happen. I do not mean that you don't make adjustments and grow beyond certain ideas and ways in which you function. I do, however, mean that there should be a set of conditions that are invaluable and thus, needed to maintain and sustain desired outcomes of a healthy and whole relationship. A few questions that I found myself asking consistently are:

- *What do I really want? What do I need to accept? Where can I adjust?*
- *Where have I grown?*
- *Am I becoming more of who God says I am? Am I changing for the better?*

Many times, our terms and conditions are based on superficial ideas, societal norms, or even religious rhetoric. I find that to be a controlling factor in how we function in the way we relate and with whom we relate, but it leaves the most important people out of the equation which are YOU and GOD. What God desires of you can foundationally look like another person, if they are following the will of God for His people and abiding by His principle. Truth be told, though, what God has in mind for you is really tailored for you. As much as I look like my mom and can pass for her in a line up, there is a distinction in my being me. There is no one else like you. That is something to smile about. This pursuit of relational healthy relationships can get heavy, but don't miss the beauty of it. Loving you completely and connecting with someone that feels the same about themselves, but also feels the same about you is just AMAZING. So, breathe. All of you deserve to be at the table and there is a chair awaiting your beauty, flaws, failures, fears and **ALL. THAT MAKES YOU BEAUTY FULL.**

BEYOND THE

Celebration

DOMONIQUE S. WASHINGTON

This is the part of life where things get a little sketchy. I know that we have all been to this place and gotten discouraged. This is the place where I need you more open and honest than you have been as we have journeyed through the pathway of collecting data with the intent to gain a lasting connection with another. So, as a warning, I am letting you know now that you may cry during this chapter. Yes, you will cry, not because I am going to damage your ego with truth that will hurt your feelings, but because I am going to expose some truth and heals some areas that you have closed off for some time, or determined altogether to never let anyone know that scar exist. This is the truth behind every woman that wants to be "chose." I want you to begin with the truth being, YOU ARE NOT THE ONLY ONE. I realize that has become a common theme throughout this body of work, but its real. YOU ARE NOT THE ONLY ONE. As crazy as your encounters have been, I can assure you there is a woman across the globe who has either come out of that same thing, is currently approaching it, or trying to determine how she cannot enter into it. It may not be identical but believe me when I tell you it is very similar. Do not allow the enemy of shame and fear to have you in turmoil, unwilling to release the pain of your encounter. Do not allow the enemy to keep you from healing a deep wound, thinking it's too crazy, silly, farfetched or outright embarrassing to share with another. No honey, I need you to rid yourself of that idea because I need that pain to be exposed so you can heal. God cannot heal what you hide. Suppressing it and pretending that it never happened doesn't make it go away either. God said to resist the devil and he will flee. Resist, in this context didn't mean to avoid, it meant to expose and face. We are getting ready to expose and face somethings. You may even find yourself needing to pause and breathe through this one. And that is ok. You cannot get to where you desire to be if you are pained by where you have been. That is how we find ourselves with the new guy. Unfortunately, many of us treat the new guy as if the old one was staring us in the face. We want to let him in, but there's someone else who hasn't been moved out of the way. You have a stand in where a new character needs to be. It's time to be free of that thing. I know it hurt. I know that you have a justifiable reason to hold on those memories. I know you loved him. I know it was good to you, but I also see how it has bounded you from truly receiving what is rightfully yours.

Let's Be Honest

Let's just be honest. Upon meeting the "guy," or in this case, "the frog," there were both conscious and subconscious ideas that this could be it. Then there is this moment upon "kissing" or in other words encountering "the frog" that you realize he wasn't the prince you had in mind. For many, this can leave you devastated and probably in the headspace of thinking one of two things:

1. I will never be hurt like that again

2. This next will be my last.

Those can seem like harmless statements to make. It can even seem like a healthy way by which to operate, but if not done with the right heart posture, being of sound mind and heart, then the right thing will quickly become the toxic thing. Let me make it personal, as to give you a break from these jabs I'm throwing.

Guilty Until Proven Innocent

After emerging from my 12 steps of grief and healing without explanation, apology, or closure, I thought I was ready to mix and mingle with the world. I was healed, but I didn't know the residue of that pain resided in a small corner of my heart. You see, the pain I experienced was so heavy for me that knowing that it was over after prayer, counsel, and time, made me think that I was just ready. My guards seemed down. My heart appeared open. My will looked ready, but was I wrong! After my broken heart, I knew that there was no way I could be the same. I was a new woman with a fresh attitude and cheerful spirit. I was ready to give out my number and post some cute selfies. But a phone conversation floored me.

After several phone calls and me listening, engaging, and enjoying this journey, I had a call with my friend who asked, "Do you realize what you are doing?" In my mind, I was thinking she was about to applaud me, but she didn't. She continued, "Do you realize what you are saying?" Annoyed, I said, "Just say what you mean." She informed me that I had an undertone of distrust. I was saying I was open. I had all of the functions of an open-hearted woman, but I had the tone of a woman scorned. I was listening to him tell his truth all the while receiving it as lies. It was as if he was guilty of not living up to his truths until there was something that was done, and or said, that made me believe him. After getting off of the phone with him, God convicted me and said, "Until you let me heal the corner of distrust in your heart, men will spend their time proving their innocence to you for a lie they will never get the chance to tell. You hear their truth but accept them as lies because of what he did. Let me heal you so you do not harm them." I felt two ways. On one hand, I was mad, because I knew that meant I could not converse with the guy anymore until God finished dealing with me, and lowkey, I was just ready to date. On the other hand, I was disappointed because I thought I had done all the "right" things to make God, and others, proud of the woman that was healed. Then it hit me. There was no need to be disappointed, because it was the job of us as humans to need the potter's touch. I will never be without flaws, but I can get to a place of living with less of them. I also had to accept this truth because it was only going to assist me in not self- sabotaging any other dating prospects because this was just too major of a step to miss.

Don't Be Anxious

I then realized that I could not be so anxious to have something that I was willing to not just accept every man, but also present myself as some woman that I was not. So ready to live out the "back in the water" chapter of life, that I was about to dive in before the water was set for me. Thinking back on that truth I am so glad God used my friend to call me out. I was travelling in uncharted waters and was about to mix and mingle with a set of men I was not ready for. You see, when on the journey to connect with others you must be mindful of what part of you is speaking in your encounters. It is very possible to be so excited about meeting a guy that you don't realize which part of you he's speaking to, and before you know it, you both have bonded based on the painful history of the past. This only leads to a toxic encounter that will continue until you are healed. Yes, you can bring all of you to the table and that "all" can encompass the painful things too. Don't be that *bag lady.*

Hopefully, you've heard Erykah Badu's song concerning the above term. I will be honest and tell you that I know the tune and hook but couldn't tell you any more than that, so don't immediately go to her song just in case we are speaking from the same idea. I simply made the reference because I know she says, "bag lady" (in my Erykah Badu voice). I can't speak on Erykah much, but if by the end of my explanation we are speaking on the same thing, then please give me my props. The bag lady I'm asking you to not be is the one who not only brings in what she desires in a mate but drags in every man she's encountered along the way. This bag lady will treat every new man like the previous one, collecting data for John and using it against Roy. She may even think of It as lessons learned, not realizing she is treating them as timed served. You must be able to separate the lesson from the man in order to truly be able to experience the man you are with for who he really is. This can be a thin line because of the way our brain functions following certain encounters. For example, it took time to encounter an artist and not automatically think that an unanswered text followed by a two-hour wait until his response automatically meant he was lying. The guy from my past taught me the lesson that a potential guy in my future wasn't trying to teach. He was being honest, but I treated it as a lie because I pulled from my bag of lessons and attempted to redeem a time that I will never be able to. I will never be able to show the old guy what I'd learned because I was never going to be with him again. What I did, in return, was show the new guy my hurt and he, being his mature self, called me out on it. So, we had to discuss it. You see, bag ladies don't hide as much as we would think. Someone who sees differently will see it and wonder "who hurt you." Hopefully, this question is being asked in an honest, concerning way that lets you know "your bag is showing and not in a narcissistic way. Don't bring a bunch of stuff you accepted from the last guy and give to the next one without any rhyme or reason. Empty your bag lady!

It All Seemed So Different

Through conversations with God, my friend, and a counselor, I searched scripture, books, and my heart to regain my trust. I learned to accept the WHO I was talking to at the time and not HEAR the who I had encountered from my past. I literally would tell myself, before answering the phone, "This is _____ (fill in the blank). He is not the pain of my past. He is his own man and until he shows me otherwise, I hear and accept his truths. This does not mean I ignore any flags. Over time I could speak to him without having to remind myself of those facts, but until I had gotten to a place of full acceptance, that phrase was my mental reminder of how to function. This is vital for anyone who has dealt with a relationship with the intent of it being a forever. If you don't allow yourself to fully heal, learn to trust again, and see the next person for who they actually are, you can find yourself having them jump through hoops, over barriers, and break down walls that they didn't even build. Look at it like this, imagine going on a vacation in 2020 without unpacking your suitcase of the last vacation in 2018. It will seem like you have more space, but in the end your making room where you could just start fresh. Some trips are just easier to pack for with an empty bag. Be sure to unpack before each new trip:

- Utilize your close circle and wisdom counsel to be honest with the encounter and how it impacted your life

- Note the places and spaces that need to be given to God, and or, a counselor to be healed

- Purpose to take the necessary time to work through all loose ends and needs to move on in a healthy way

- Accept, adjust and agree with the birth of a new normal

- Commit to being consistent with vowing to function from your healed space

- Keep in mind that where you are headed is a new space and does not need the old being brought into it.

Unpacking the old to enter healthily into the new is so important. Don't miss this step. It wasn't until I stopped being miserable with who I had become that I was able to be mesmerized by who I had become. Pain birthed a new woman.

Here We Grow Again

I had unpacked someone beautiful that was truly ready to venture off into the future. Now that the heavy stuff is out of the way, let's get to some fun facts.

Every frog isn't your Prince.

Listen Lady, Now, that you are ready to start collecting data from men I need you to know that **EVERY MAN YOU MEET IS NOT THE MAN YOU MATE.** Have you ever just stopped and realized that God can send a MAN to be a friend to you as well? It is possible to connect with the male gender as a friend and it not come from being put in a "zone." We have to get out of this mindset of seeing male and thinking mate. He can be cute, saved, a little hood, like you like, the right height, nice car, house and credit score and still not be the mate at the end of the rainbow. Have you ever stopped and asked God, "who is he to me," before you place him where you think he should be? He is a man, yes. He is good husband material, I'm sure. He's talking right, I know.

But none of those things automatically make him the mate God had in mind for you. Sometimes we need to just pause and ask God before we start sizing him up. I can be honest and say that's not an "easy" place to be in, but I can also be honest and say asking God first and not seeing him as "the mate" too soon can save you a lot of heartache, time and pain.

Eat a snicker. I love the outrageous snickers commercials that have a character behaving in a crazy way and then it says, You're not that hungry. Eat a Snickers. *Women of God, we have to stop being so desperate that we just looking dumb.*

Yes, I said it. We know we don't want a man with kids. We meet a man with 5 kids, 3 baby mommas, no Jesus, and then get caught up in a space that neither our education, grandmother, or God raised us to be and then leave it up to "being led on." No honey, my God didn't do that. You let society, a friend, your heart, or your hormones lead you there. That situation lacked intelligence before it started. Before you get caught up in a need for a man, let me tell you what my daddy told me. Go to JCPenney and get a pair of 32 long pants and hang them up in the closet before you get yourself in that kind of mess. The intent was for you to laugh, but I'm also serious. There are some good things that can come from our desperation, i.e. the woman with the issue of blood.

But there are also some not so good things that can come from our desperation, such as when Sarah gave Hagar to Abraham.

Make it plain. It's easy to fall prey to adjusting who you are because you want to be "chose." Don't do that. Make your expectation known in the boldest and yet subtle way possible. I'm not saying to sit at the table and pull out your scroll of all your needs, but I am saying to be open to insert your expectations, do's/don'ts, will's/won'ts as data is being released. Imagine this, you meet a man out of state, and he says you must fly to him. It is your truth that you are uncomfortable with that idea and would rather an initial meeting be done in your state. MAKE THAT PLAIN. Everything is worthy of a mature, healthy conversation.

Listen as much as you speak. When collecting data, you have to remember that you are not just on the issuing end, but you are also on the receiving end. Express your desires, but also take the time to LISTEN to the desires of the other person. Not to become who they desire, but to be sure that he, too, gets what he desires as well.

He's just not that into you: Don't ignore the signs. We do not have to suffer rejection. Listen with your ears and not your heart. Men are pretty simple, often. When he tells you what he isn't ready for, BELIEVE him. It's ok to exit stage left and not have to be escorted out.

It ain't all bad. Things don't have to be sour to no longer be sweet. Just because something didn't end the way you desired doesn't mean things have to end in a negative space. You can agree to not pursue and move on without malice. It doesn't mean you have to remain friends, but it does mean that it's ok if you don't.

Just breathe. Collecting data is a serious matter, but it should also be enjoyable. Why are you stressed out and strained after the third conversation? Lighten up a bit. After being single for a while, don't you just want to smile at your phone for once? Don't take all of the fun out of the encounter by trying to run down the aisle. Take a brisk walk through the day and see if the sun hits his melanin like you like it before you plan out engagement pictures. (LOL).

Those are just a few of the things that we should look toward and forward too after the initial encounter. We must learn to live in such a space that we can survive beyond the celebration before we plan one.

DOMONIQUE S. WASHINGTON

RELATIONAL
Intelligence

DOMONIQUE S. WASHINGTON

There is an innate space within all of us to connect with another. I want to encourage your heart to know emphatically that there is nothing wrong with your desire to connect with someone. I recall a time when I prayed to God asking him to remove the desire for companionship if he was not going to send someone to fill it. Thinking back on it, I am glad he did not answer that prayer, because when he does send my mate, I will not need that added work of "wanting" what I had been waiting for all this time. So, if you were like me trying to close yourself off to not want to feel the desire for another, rethink that one.

At the point of collecting data from another you get to a place of wanting more. It is all fun and games until you get to the day that you are awakened with this strong need to connect to YOUR person. You are, to an extent, over meeting people, realizing it is not anything lasting, and letting it go. You want more. More consistency, steady and solid, so that you can just grow and be. This is where we must be careful. This is the day that we need to feel that desire but not give it a chance to lead. Although there is a need for us to connect with others there should not be an obsession to fill that need with a relationship or marriage.

Every connection has its own level of importance to fill that space that God placed in all of us. In Genesis, He did create Eve to fulfill this "need" in Adam; however, before there was Eve, God had himself in the Garden with Adam, followed by some animals that helped him fulfill purpose of fatherhood by having to name, protect, and nurture them. That is a topic for an entirely different book, but hopefully, you get my drift. The desire for another does not have to solely be filled by man. That desire can be filled in other forms and will be filled in its own time. You have time. Stop thinking that you need to rush to this ultimate connection because of a time clock that is running out, or you are just over where you are. Just as there is a time and season for everything that is a place for every person. Do not rush to relate. That can seem easier said than done, but in all honesty, it is. It is all based on your perspective. In this chapter, we are going to acknowledge our "people" and put them in the right place for our lives. We will think from both a present day and future life. All our engagement and involvement should be meaningful from the friends that we surround ourselves with to the person that we give our heart to. Each one has a role to play. It is our responsibility to put everyone in the space that is fit for them.

There's Levels to This Thing

After you identify that the data you have collected is enough to continue a pursuit there are a few things that should be in place. **First**, you want to be sure that there is someone that can be an objective, and yet, compassionate person by which you expose this connection to in a hopes that you can trust them enough to be unbiased and honest in what they see in this person. Imagine having this person to meet the person that you are intentionally dealing with and having communicated with them that you would like to have them in the person of this potential mate in hopes that they pick up, from a spiritual level, their spirit (vibe), how you behave when you around them, ask a few leading questions to create a conversation and explore their view/stance/heart in areas that you could have missed etc. The point of this interaction is to help you SEE where your view could have been based on your desire, the initial excitement of beginning a connection often identified as the fairytale phase, as well as having someone that knows you to gaze into the potential of this situation from a different point of view. This does not mean that what they have to say has the final wait. It does however intend to be some more data to take with you as you journey through interactions and encounters with another. Now, I understand this is not as common as it should be. The reason I say "should be" is because I found, in my own experience, that the person/people that you expose the initial engagement with need to more than excited that you found someone. They need to be people that can be excited for where you are, but have an open mind to see the nature of the encounter, toxic or healthy, caliber of person you are connecting with, honest or playing, and the nature in which you are journeying, running shoes are all in.

As I am asking you to put this person in this place, I also need you to consider where they are. It is important, **secondly**, that you are mindful of where your advice is coming from. Essentially, people can only advise you from where they are and where they've been. Where they've been will help them to encourage you in the space of what not to do, or what has been done based upon what has or hasn't worked. Where they are is simply being able to advice from their exact position. This is where things can get a bit tricky. Their current state of relating in their personal life, be it healthy, whole, growing, toxic, unforgiving, bitter etc. is exactly where they will speak from. It took me a minute to realize this fact. I found myself getting a lot of my advice from someone that had more experience than me in dating. That was good for my initial space of collecting data, but when my data begin to grow in the area of intentionally relating, I found the potential harm in continuing to use their advice in the space I was in. *When it comes to advice, it is simply an opinion to consider at the deliberation table, but it does not have to be your end-all unless it is a source that has been qualified through God with prayer and guidance.* My source of advice did not change when the nature of my interaction did. Because the function of her current relationship was intense and continuing to function.

When I found myself at the space of "seeing flags," the advice I received was subconsciously encouraging me to do the same. I was attempting to collect data from this guy that was showing signs of places and spaces that were unhealthy. His stories just didn't add up sometimes. For instances, there was an incident when he said that he missed a flight to see me, but the screenshot that he sent me to verify this only confirmed the truth that the flight was in fact delayed but not that he purchased a ticket.

I decided to consider the advice and continue relating because the voice of the advice disqualified my own. This was not her fault; it was mine. You see, because I had come out of a terrible relationship, I did not trust me to know how to "properly" collect data. This led me into not trusting my own voice, signs and or emotions. I was relating solely on the voice that was reason in the beginning stages, not realizing as the stages increased, I needed to look position my "person" again. It is ok to not use the same voice in one area that you would in another. I am not saying to have so many speaking in your ear and advancing your interactions. I am saying, however, that if the "source of advice" does not or cannot cover the full spectrum of a healthy relationship from beginning to end then it is ok to use certain people for certain places. This is all a part of putting people in their place.

Just as you would identify in a social setting what friend is good for knowing restaurants and hotel with travel and who would know the latest songs on the radio you can also qualify who is good with sound advice, getting you to go to God in prayer, checking you when you are dead wrong and seeing when you cannot.

Which leads to my **final** thought of your need to put the right people in the right place so that you are pulling on the right people for the right things. If your main friend cannot be trusted for the main things, then consider that they may need to be moved into a different place. That may mean that the high school buddy no longer fits the purpose driven you. That is scary to admit, but it may be a scary you need to face. The people we connected to are not just for our past or present, but we must begin to see the importance of placement for our future. Does your future self-benefit from the connection that were once made by your past self? Can your present self- benefit more by letting go of things that "were" and connecting to things that are to come? Moving forward with clear intent can be an exciting adventure, but it does have its uncomfortable spaces. Be sure that the people you pull on in both times are those that will not only encourage enjoyment, but properly enlighten the tough space of making this level of an encounter. If the right people are in the right spaces it may not be perfect, but it will be helpful as you further navigate through creating a healthy foundation and space as you build the walls of relating to and connecting with another. I want to give that "heavy" bit of information a chance to resonate as we go into the lighter topic of social media.

Post to Be vs. Supposed to Be

Girl meets guy. Guy and girl decided to collect data exclusively. Guy and or girl want the world to know about this "data" being collected. At least one person (or maybe both girl and guy) wants to use the only outlet that lets the world know what's up; social media. Be it a post for the gram or telling the book of faces, this is a moment of decision that we all will openly or secretly face, to post or not to post that is the BIG question. I would have been remised to be speaking on relational intelligence and not address the biggest elephant in the room of social media. I have seen, as I am sure you have, the meme's about posting to early, not enough or not at all. I am sure that you have both read them as well as nodded your head to them as truth however, I would like you to open your mind to qualifying those memes with a perspective that voids them of their factuality for your life and your ability to nod in agreeance but not accept them into your situation. You see, when it comes to having a solid view as to how you will act, agree to act and or desire to act in a situation that you are not in yet you have the tendency to come into alignment with a truth that can change based on where you are in life and to whom you are traveling with. The younger you may have wanted to be private out of fear of rejection. The healed you may want to be public because you have had an understanding based on a communicated expectation and agreeing to stand in your truth for your journey. It is very important that when considering communicating expectations, desires and how you will function on your exclusive intended journey of collecting data that you not only vocalize what is desired but you are sure that there has been an agreement by both parties from a healed and whole why. Ask yourself and each other why do we want this and what will it mean? Expectations need to not just be put on the table, but they need to be mutually agreed upon at different phases of your journey. Even Netflix has showed us this to be true. Have you been watching a show on Netflix and after so long they ask if you are still watching the show you told them you wanted to watch? This is their way of being sure that you are STILL committed to the process of the choice you made to watch this series. That is the same way you need to be when traveling on the road of data collecting exclusively. This is vital to how we function in culture and for the climate of our connections. Do not think that there is a way that this part of your travel is supposed to be posted. I have been given the advice that information should "be private, but not a secret." Although I feel that to be solid advice, I found it to filter off into yet another trend of this idea of supposed to be. I like to say it like this: Make sure the concrete is solid before you walk on it because if not you leave a print to let others have a visual and conversation about where you left your tracks.

Going Public

Going public has to do with opening a connection up in both the actual eye of the public of close friends, family, and frequent group of social interaction i.e. extended families, church families and maybe even a work environment. It also details opening a connection up to the public via social media. We must begin to be mindful of the very fact that going public opens your connections up to both public opinion and a possible subconscious need for public approval. It's one thing to be excited and wanting to share your journey to the world. There is nothing wrong with a mutual decision to do that from a healthy why. I would like to submit for your consideration to be mindful that doing so can have both a positive and negative impact. This is due to the very fact that intentional connections have both high and low points. Keeping that in mind it is during the high points that people celebrate your journey and may have even created a hashtag of having it as a goal for health and wholeness. You may hear and or see things like "Y'all look cute together," #RelationshipGoals, oh and this is a good love for the kingdom. All of those seem positive and harmless however they can go from well wishes to pressure as the likes on your post increase. Not only does it mean they will applaud your journey it also means that those exposed to the lows. This exposure can happen via assumption when no posting is happening, to consumption when a lot of information is given concerning the journey or presumption based on a possible exposure from a conversation had with a trusted other. It doesn't take much for people to think they should have an opinion during this era however it is more probable that they assumed opinion become vocal when people can assume they have a right to said opinion because you made it public by posting in a public space. I am not saying any of this to discourage you in a direction. I simply want you to be mindful of the effects that publicity can give. Should you go public begin to have a conversation about how you will respond to such things and how you will troubleshoot its effect on your journey overall.

Hype It Up

All this exposure leads to some hype. There is some excitement that comes with being a trending topic, inspiration and talk of the church house (insert slight laugh). Just as much as you can be excited keep in mind that there are some petty betty's and angry joes awaiting the I told you so from the fellowship hall. Try not to fall into the idea that you need to put on for the sake of who knows as well as not using social media to humiliate, address or expose your issue with the person that you have agreed to collect data from. Have a solid stance for dealing with the speed bumps and roadblocks.

I recall first learning how to drive. I was driving through a parking lot with a speed bump and for whatever reason I didn't think back to the driving handbook's advice to drivers to slow down upon approaching it and going over it slightly. I just kept at my same driving space and before I knew it the tail end of my car went up and my brother was in the back smiling as if he had ridden his favorite roller coaster. That may have been fun for my brother, but it was a shocker for me. So much so that the next time I approached a speed bump I had a solid plan. I went back to the handbook and refreshed myself on what I should have done. Had a laugh with my mom who jokingly gave me advice on what she does when she sees a speedbump. This had me more confident and prepare on how to handle the next one when it would come along. I was not sure when I would see it, but I was prepared for whenever I did. That is exactly how I would encourage you to be on your journey to intentional connecting. Be sure you have a plan for the bumps you know of and create a plan after facing the places you didn't know and or consider to be an issue going forward. You will not know it all however, being in the age of getting informed you have to go back and recall the information you did take in and have a plan on how you will approach it the next time it comes. With this book I just gave you either insight, inspiration, or new information on how to face social media when it comes up. Now you have yet another thing to consider when you get to the committed phase of your dating life.

A Queen to Be

Yes, collecting data should be taken seriously, but creating data can also be done in a way that does not feel like interviewing for a five-star restaurant with world renown owners. I know you are a full course meal that will not be found anywhere else in America. Work that truth sis. Just try to be the woman that owns that truth while being the Queen that presents it in a way that does not have to be yelled to be heard. I took a liking to the Royal family following the last Royal Wedding and one thing I found is that the Queen does not need to announce herself to be respected. Her presence alone speaks more volume than a loud speaker ever will. Oh, but when she speaks the boldness of her stance fills a room. She knows her authority. She is mindful of the power her words are in creating the Kingdom that she lives in. She knows there are others effected by her decision. She is not only possessed and powerful, but she is filled with purposeful passion. There are things along her journey that she could not change just as well as there were things along her journey that she had to change. Queen, yes, I am referring to you now, when you take the throne of solidifying your place in another person's life be sure that you consider how you want to be seen by God, yourself and your future mate. Queens move differently. Live as such. Relate as such. Try not to just demand from your encounters but place a command in your encounters. There is a major difference. A demand is to request forcefully while a command is to compel and direct with authority. Being intelligent in your relations is taking all the knowledge that you have collected and using it to create wise encounters to create more healthy and progressive advancement. The throne of relating with wisdom is yours for the sitting. Use what you already have in your possession as well as what information you are continuing to collect to make the best out of every relationship you dock.

MEANINGFUL

Investment

DOMONIQUE S. WASHINGTON

It was a Tuesday morning, and I had a plan of running the list of errands that I had put off on the weekend. I got dressed and grabbed my keys with the intent to drive in the direction to reach the places I wanted to go. I put the keys in the ignition, but I just sat there. And as I sat in my car, I began to get distracted with my phone, a few emails, and why my USB cord would not connect to the Bluetooth. Here I was, dressed in good intentions, in a mode of transportation with a desired destination, and yet, I had not really started the car or opened the garage to actually begin my journey. Someone in the house would have assumed I was ready to go and would not take up too much time to get there. I did make the announcement of where I wanted to be and grabbed my keys as if I was headed there, but once the door closed and I got to the car what I announced to do and what actually took place were extremely different. It is one thing to say where you want to be, and it is altogether different to look the part having never proceeded to the route. Therefore, it is important to speak on making a meaningful investment in your connections. Do not just put your time and attention anywhere and hope to get somewhere. The desire is not enough to drive the car.

The passengers do not mean you are going to automatically be on the same page or right path. A passenger simply means that your intent was good when you started. It is the willingness to make meaningful decisions, determinations and diligent investments in the path, process and the proceeding forward intentionally are vital to the overall investment.

Let us look at those two words, meaningful and investment. Meaning means having a distinctiveness. In other words, it is putting a precise, exact definition to something. So, to be meaningful is to be full of preciseness. When you look at meaningful in terms of collecting data, this is where you move from assumption to vocalization. In this phase of being a data agent, there should be concise communication taking place. I have found that too many single people do not ask enough questions out of fear of asking too many questions, or keeping things light to be more appealing. This never ends well.

The fear of assuming can lead to a bit of pain. Pain for you if you were to assume that if you verbalize a desired end, being a relationship with them, is picked up from the angle that includes you. I have heard people say, "He led me on." Upon hearing this, I ask a follow up question, "Did he lead you or did you lead yourself." I do not ask that to be mean; however, I do ask it for the person to go back and look at their conversation. Were you communicating under the guise of generalizing in an effort to not have too much meaning, or were you communicating in a precise way that will let the receiver of the information know where you are willing to invest? Some may say "I do say what I want." I would like to follow that thought up with, "Were you sure that your want is mutual?" Often without warning we have our meaning and fail to be sure the other people are meaning the same thing. Just because a person agrees to have consistent communication does not give us the right to not determine intent which makes way for meaning.

That leads us to our next word in question, investment. To invest means to allocate resources to gain a profit. In the case of a relationship, the profit is determined by the person. It is up to both parties involved, and the end goal of the data collecting is to determine what results both parties are seeking. In most cases, the assumed end goal is marriage; however, many need to open their minds to the idea that to assume an end goal of said parties involved is a hopeful endeavor. It is, in my opinion, to be sure to not only inquire, but to also adhere to the spoken and agreed upon goal of both data agents. Too often we hear the phrase "I'm not ready for the relationship" and yet we think that because of the time that they agree to spend and the conversations that consistently have, that data will be irrelevant because the words and action must be an investment. What I have found is that when an investment is intended the parties have weighed the cost using all pre and post data to make a quality decision that communication would not interfere with. An investment is a commitment. It is best to allow words and actions to agree. To not allow the emotions you are building with a person to repaint the picture they handed you in the beginning of your involvement. Unless a change is directly stated between two parties, it is better to believe the initial dialogue than it is to assume that the turn in the road of conversation will get you to the destination you secretly desire. That's it. Secret desires can go unfilled. Blatant disregard for the truth of someone's words can cause pain. It may sound harsh but we as women have to remember that we are wired differently from men and yet we both can desire the same end results. I heard a man say that we as women should believe what they say. That their actions are only indentation of them thinking that what they said was considered and the woman still decided to invest knowing the truth. KNOW THE TRUTH. Biblically speaking we hear "the truth will set us free" and although there are many instances where this scripture has been taken out of context I would like you to consider using the words of the decree for the impact that it has when you think it and say it aloud. KNOW THE TRUTH, BELIEVE THE TRUTH and THAT TRUTH that you adhere to will SET YOU FREE from anything contrary to it. When someone TELLS you what they want BELIEVE them.

Recognize the Truth

I know what you are thinking. You are asking the same question I asked myself. How will I know beyond words that someone is investing in me based upon the data that both parties are collecting? I am going to discuss a few truths of an investment:

Truth 1: A good investment is properly weighed on both sides. Investing can sound like a complicated space to qualify. Many people are just killing time. Going around professing to collect data from several spaces in hopes of narrowing it down to one has caused a plethora of pain and problems for both the male and female. This is where dating always got a little uncertain for me. I am not the person that needs to shop around publicly to make a permanent decision on what I want. I have never needed to test drive any vehicle I have owned to solidify my purchase. I am the type who said, "I see what I want, now let's count the cost, work the numbers, to see if it's in my budget to do so." Counting the costs allows me to operate from a place that will not cause strain or stress trying to maintain. I have found this to not go over well with salesmen or men that were not serious about what they wanted. The social system will make you think you HAVE to test drive and shop around publicly to know what you REALLY want. That idea has also shaped our dating life. For believers, especially, this can potentially lead to more problems than a few, as it contradicts not only your heart posture, but also your heart's desire. This can lead you being with men that you know you see no real future with just to fulfill this superficial need to SEE more as if the more you see will change what you saw. What I have found to be true is that the more you see will have you finding more ways to alter what you saw to make it fit. When you are sure of what you want you can determine how much farther you are willing to go to close the deal. There is no sense in investing in a place that either does not meet the minimum desire or is not doing anything to attempt becoming what the both of you are seeking.

A relational investment should be seen from both ends. There should be two people willing to see two people in a frame rather than only one. Imagine standing in an elongated mirror. For some time, only one person could fit in its frame. That is until the one person that it has always been decides to move over, just a tad, to get the other person in view. That is what a mutual investment should look like. Being willing to give up a full space to fit another in the space knowing that they are doing the same on their end. Making things work and to come to a common ground for the overall whole.

Remember the car dealership I mentioned earlier? I knew what I wanted, we sat down and worked the numbers until we found a place that both the dealership and I could agree to without it being too heavy on one side. Before I got in the car to see how it drives, I needed to be sure that the place of purchase would be willing to move over just a little so that I could have a sense of peace as we worked out the deal. When I saw that they were willing to change a few numbers and percentages, I knew that I could proceed with the deal. A good investment, a good relationship, is when you can see a win on both sides.

Truth 2: An investment is based upon the facts of the data collected. I have seen people attempt to make an investment based upon the idea of a thing while ignoring the reality of it. People have stayed in relationships that lacked the true nature and character of the person they desired thinking that if they show that they are invested, the foundation of a person will change. That is a very dangerous idea to continue to conform to. One thing I learned while collecting data is that you will never be good enough or powerful enough to change someone. People adjust and change because they want to change. If they want to change, you will not have to wonder if they are changing. You will see and hear the want in how they communicate and behave. Investing with meaning in a person that lacks trust, passion, love, and those foundational things that you need and desire to have in your relationship based on a wish is setting yourself up for doom. Invest with the facts. Pay attention to the numbers and verbiage before. To draw more into the car analogy--investing in a relationship that lacks the fuel to keep it going is like sitting in a car believing that it will move if you merely wish for the lack of fuel to change. You can stay in that car wishing if you want, but gas will not manifest. You can stay with that person if you want, but who you want them to be will not manifest. A wish turned reality is about doing the work. Unless the driver is willing to get out and get the gas is available, but not useful.

Truth 3: An investment should gain value over time, not lose it. When thinking of a relational investment and it is gaining value over time think in terms of asset over debt. An asset is something that is useful and therefore deemed valuable. The value is determined by the individual. You must ask yourself, "what do I gain by being in connection with this person?" Yes, you are going to ask yourself how this connection benefits, enhances, grows, and overall affects your life for the better. The more you get to know about someone the more you get to see how their being is going to have an impact on your life in either a giving or taking way. Consider this, the more I was connected to this person, the more I realized that he was not good with money. Not only was he not good at handling his own money, but I later found that he was not good in keeping his word concerning money. Realizing that truth left me with a choice of whether I should continue to invest time and energy in a relationship knowing that it will be a financial burden. For some, this may sound harsh, but whether you say it aloud or not this is where you find yourself when dealing with investing in others. From this place, it is safe to draw the conclusion that your connections can either be an asset or a liability. The more you get to see someone interact and engage in their day to day life the more you get to see how much value you want to place on them. It does not mean that you disrespect them openly, or you do not try to influence them to take a chance. It does, however, mean that you consider the truth of the matter and go in with the idea that I am going to gain or lose based on continuing in this union. If I decide to continue to move knowing there is more of a chance of acquiring debt than experiencing a gain I must be satisfied with that choice. Let us go back to our car analogy. Have you ever heard of buying a lemon? This is a term used in the car industry to describe making an investment in a car that turns out to have several defects that affect the safety, value, and overall utility of the car. This is not usually a car that is based on sight and the initial test drive to have these issues. It is a car that after some time will begin to fall apart. It looks like a good car. It drove like a good car, but, over time, the truth of the matter begins to show. As time goes on, you begin to see that any further investment in getting this car to function in that way that you invested your money, time and effort for it to function is a waste. There is no return that will be given on this investment where it is. No time. No money. No mechanic can change the foundational issues under the hood. At least not in a way that you need the car to drive. This is where I want you to go back to when determining the value of your investment. Is there more gain or give as time goes on? Am I willing to continue to invest seeing what I see and knowing what I know? Can the life I desire to have make it through if things never change?

Truth 4: An investment should not be measured solely on highs. Because life is not filled with highs alone it should not be expected for relational investments to be. Many times, we decide to continue in connecting based upon a high emotional pull that the person has on us. They make me feel good or I am happy when I am with them. This is all good, but would you still be with them if the butterflies and gumdrops leave? When the smile fades and the initial excitement is over, would you still invest? There is a show on Netflix where they remodel old cars and basically flip them to big money deals. The guys on the show are aware of how much money they have the potential to make with each rebuild; however, there are times that they know that getting to that place will cost them big and may not automatically produce the desired results. But they count on the cost. If the end game will be beneficial for their financial advancement, then they continue in the deal knowing that truth. You, too, should consider the same. Will this investment benefit me in a progressively positive and meaningful way, or will I lose more if I continue to invest now?

Truth 5: An investor must have the capacity to contain the investment. I have heard it stated by a psychologist that humans are containers. This idea caused me to research that now truth. A container is anything that has the capacity to hold or contain something. Every container has a capacity level that determines how much of something it can hold. Capacity has to do with the maximum amount that something can hold. As an investor it is important to know two things, how much room do you have to hold and how much did you begin with to give out. It is very important, at the start of an investment, that you determine how much you have in you to take in. People come with the need to both give and release. If you do not have the capacity to take in as much as the investment needs than you will find yourself worn out and overwhelmed. An investor is consistently mindful and clear in stating how much more they have to give as well has being sure to be clear on what they need to be filled. If the investment does not have the capacity to meet your fill level in the beginning, then one must consider that continuing to give toward the investment will have you upside down on your loan. They will owe you more than the value of the investment. If we take it back to the car analogy imagine going on a four- hour road trip knowing that it takes a full tank of gas to get to the destination and back without running out. But this time instead of filling the car up, knowing the truth, you decided to only put a half of a tank of gas in the car. This may sound silly, but it's real. You knew what was needed to have a successful trip without running out of gas. You knew the capacity that the tank needed to be filled to make it to your destination and back and yet you only filled the tank to the halfway mark. This would mean that you will have enough gas to get to your destination, but not enough to get from your destination. This is where we seem to fail. We know what is needed. We know what we need to be filled. We admit the truth of the person not having the capacity to carry what we possess and yet we invest anyway. There are times that not brushing people off for where they are not is admirable however, there are times where we tend to hold who people really are against them because they don't live up to where we need them to be. This can create an unsafe environment for growth. We have to start being real within ourselves first and being mindful of where those around us are so that we can stop demanding things that maybe someone can't or do not have the desire or skill set to fill. Ask yourself "do they have the capacity to hold what I carry and vice versa.

The reason it is vital to consider all the truths is because when all is said and done a true meaningful investment says I saw the facts and I will be comfortable and still move forward with you should you never become who I think you should. Yes, I said it. When a meaningful investment is on the table the investor has considered all truths and is willing to stand by them. All truths do not just include the pleasurable ones, but the not so great ones too. Most people begin to experience this level of engagement and because it does not mimic their favorite Hollywood movie, they want a refund. Real investment can slowly begin to be given the title of love. Love does not look like the highlight reel of your favorite movie. Real love causes you to feel free to uncover the scars you have hidden and reveal the truths unknown. The objective is to feel comfortable enough to be completely naked but have the trust that the revealing will not expose to the point of abuse (miss use). You see, the meaningful investments that last a lifetime consider the now and make way for the later. Accepting patterns but being committed to reveal areas of growth while coaching and encouraging reaching them. How comforting it can be to be riding in the car with the destination in mind looking over at the passenger with you knowing that not only are we in the same car wanting to get to the same place, but we are both willing to put in the same effort to ensure that we get there together. I gain and give knowing that you will do the same. *Move with meaning or just stand still.*

BE THEE

Happy

DOMONIQUE S. WASHINGTON

There will come a time in your life that you are full of so much bliss that you will want to make a caption that reads "Finally Happy." Yes, your story seems to finally be making a break for marital bliss. All the angels are rejoicing, and heaven finally sent the person that God had designed for you. Be it your initial shot at love or your second chance. There will be a day that things begin to "look up" but want you to consider not looking at it as a FINALLY. Reason begin is that through the journey of my first book, Ever After Happily, you learned that the fairytale begins and ends with you. With this book is my prayer that you realized how many joys that can come with things a narrow perspective will alone align to sorrow. That you can smile during every phase of your lives journey to love. That not only will it grow you, but it will meet you where you are and take you where you desire to be if you let it. That would mean that instead of finally, as an end all, you understand the power in your possession of just being all. Our forever first lady coined this idea as BECOMING and I would like to agree with her on the BE part of the phrase. The more you BE the more you are. Not just BE in the sense of coming alive and accepting flaws but BEING in the form of existing to live out the growth and work that the journey of life will take. Life is not only decision driven but it is work driven. We must be willing to be diligent in the work that it takes to develop into not only the person we desire to be but the person that is to be desired. Here is a question I ask often, "Are you the person that the person you are looking for is looking for?" With that thought in mind you must learn to consistently find the joy and the love of the journey and mark the spot of happy and not just leave it as an open space for some person to fill.

Not Their Job

It is not the job of another wandering soul to fill the shoes of happiness for another. Although us human containers have the capacity to fill a lot of holes in the story of life concerning another, it is not our job nor ability to BE THE HAPPY that they need. Because we are all on a journey and figuring out life through lessons of weakness and strengths there will be a time that I will be the source of pain when I do not want to. If happy only comes from another than misery will be your comfort. We humans are too frail to consistently fill that space. I can be the reason for the moment but not the consistent sustainer. That just cannot be a title that one can live up to. It is going to be very important to take some time to yourself to go within yourself and operate in purpose, the reason by which God placed you on earth, in order to have the void of joy filled in a way that no human can take away.

My sister loves a good singer. She introduced me to this Instagram star by the name of Samoht. She sent me this song titled, "I'm not God," and it was as if he read my journal. If you have not heard this song, I suggest that you listen to THIS SONG. Emphasis on the "this" because my fellow "pk" does not always have clean lyrics that the saints will approve of. Therein lies my disclaimer. Listen to more at your own discretion. Anyway, the lyrics center on his relationship and realizing that he did not have enough in him to change the person for the better. Although he desired for them to be healed, happy, and healthy, he drew the conclusion that he just was not God. I said all of that to tell you the same thing. Biblically speaking, when God mentioned joy, he did not recommend that it come solely from another. He referenced salvation, the Lord, hope, trust and even trouble, but I do not recall a verse saying that PEOPLE should be it.

God knew that if people could pass out joy, then people could take it from you at their convenience. No one person should have that much power. Giving someone else the charge over your happiness is like owning your own house and letting someone else hold the keys. You would only be allowed to enter and leave at the permission of the key holder unless you are ok with leaving everything within the house unsecure. If you would not do this with your house, do not do it with your happiness.

Step into Your Greatness

Inside of each of us is a void that only a deity can fill and yet there is a fulfillment that comes with our ability to connect one to another. Every interaction will not end in a lifelong investment with meaning and value to hold until forever, but every encounter should create in us a sense of growth and fulfillment even in the minor of accounts. Be it a smile from a stranger, text of endearment from a loved one, or the joy of just being free from the bondage that once had you bound each of us will be given the opportunity to be on the giving and receiving side of love and compassion. The joy that is the strength to endure after each phase of life's transitions will only be found in the joy that comes withstanding in the truth of exactly who you are BEING while continuing on your journey to becoming. If better than yesterday meets even better today, I say Queen, you are coming along true. True to your failures that prepared your success, the tears that water the plants grown from problems and joy unbreakable that built the trust in God that passes up everything logic and reasoning understand. Continue to give this world something to smile about. In case you did not know the something is you.

The world awaits your **BEING**.

Real Thing

Am I dreaming

Is it too surreal
To grasp the concept
Of reality turned fairytale

Are the times too different
For the golden commitment
Is it too naive
For me to agree
In purpose with another
For two hearts to truly connect
as one and create an atmosphere
conducive of worship
while living life to please the other?

Am I
Being too persistent
On pushing to get this
Old school
Forever type thing
Or was Jazmine right
Forever don't last always
Love will come
but it may not stay?

How do I
Keep hope alive
While encountering the
Hopeless state of
Our generations
Move by social media
And edited renditions of
Love?

What do I do with this
Am I setting myself up
for failure or
would I do more of failing
if I don't wait and see
if what I dream can be obtained?

The answers are simple
I see them clearly
If I'm not moved by
Where they say I should be
I have more to lose
Than to gain
By moving with the crowd
And not go against the grain
No matter the sayings, times or pain
once more
And again
Wait
You're worth it

#MyHeartSpeaksInPoetry

Printed by BoD™in Norderstedt, Germany